Rainer Krumm & Sonja Wittig

30 Minutes

Team Culture

Bibliographic information from the German National Library
The German National Library lists this publication in the German National Bibliography. Detailed bibliographic information can be found online at http://dnb.d-nb.de.

ISBN 978-3-96739-086-5

Cover design: die imprimatur, Hainburg
Cover concept: Martin Zech Design, Bremen
Editing: Happenstance Type-O-Rama, Oakland, USA
Graphics: 9 Levels Institute for Value Systems GmbH & Co KG, Ravensburg
Author's photo Krumm: Uwe Klössig, Berlin
Author's photo Wittig: Stephanie Kunde, Hürth
Set: Zerosoft, Timisoara (Romania)
Printing and processing: Print-on-demand

First published under the title "30 Minuten Teamkultur" in 2020 by GABAL Verlag, Germany

www.9levels.com

You'll know more in 30 minutes!

This book is designed to enable you to absorb concise and sound information in a short time. With the help of a guidance system, you will be led through the book. This will allow you to grasp the essentials within your personal time allotment (from 10 to 30 minutes).

Short reading time

You can read the whole book in 30 minutes. If you have less time, read only those passages that contain important information.

- **All important information is printed in grey.**

- Key questions with page references at the beginning of each chapter allow for quick orientation: you turn directly to the page that closes your knowledge gap.

- *Numerous summaries within the chapters allow for skimming.*

- The "Fast Reader" at the end of the book summarizes all important information.

- An index makes it easier to find what you are looking for.

Contents

Preface 6

1. Importance of team culture 9
Why teams often fail 10
Success through fit 14
Team culture and the 7-S model 16

2. Elements of team culture 21
Employees 22
Management 23
Skills 26
Processes 28
Structure 30
Strategy 32
Values 33

3. Levels of Team Culture 37
The Graves Model 38
The 9 Levels of Value Systems 40
Levels and team culture 45

4. Development of team culture 71
Resistance to change 72
Directions of change 73
Other value-based interventions 82

Fast Reader 89

The authors 94

Further Reading 95

Index 96

Foreword

"What values do we have as a team? How do we currently live them? And what should we adapt so that we can align our thoughts and actions even more closely with our values in the future?" These were the questions to which the newly formed executive board of a group with 50,000 employees sought answers. Actually, the board of directors wanted to deal with the values of the entire organization in a workshop—but they realized that they did not yet have a clear picture of even themselves as a team. They realized that they first had to clarify for themselves how they wanted to work together as a board and present themselves to the outside world. To do this, they first reflected on and defined their team values. In a second step, they tried, among other things, to create their processes, structure, and strategy and align them as closely as possible to these values: "What individual values does each member bring to the board? What is the core competency of our team, and where do we need to expand our skills? How do we ensure that we stay on course and succeed as a team in all of this?"

Employees, leadership, skills, processes, structure, strategy, values—these factors are part and parcel of team culture. Their design makes a team a distinctive group of people working together on a task.

Each team has these seven elements in a completely specific shape. Team culture is not static but is constantly adapting to the current circumstances and challenges in accordance with internal or external pressure for change.

In this book you will learn how to better understand and classify team culture on the basis of Professor Clare W. Graves's model of step-by-step value development. In addition, you will learn how you can consciously initiate and shape the development of a team culture—as the management team did in the example given above.

We wish you every success in recognizing and creating a team culture that fits your specific context and makes you and your team successful!

Rainer Krumm & Sonja Wittig

30 MINUTES

Why does teamwork not always lead to success?

Page 10

On which levels is fit important?

Page 14

How can the 7-S model be used to describe team cultures?

Page 14

1. The importance of team culture

"Culture eats strategy for breakfast!" This is one of the most frequently used quotes on the subject of change. It is often attributed to Peter Drucker (1909–2005), an American pioneer of modern management theory. The quote illustrates the fundamental importance of culture for organizations' prospects of success: culture plays a decisive role in determining what the people involved think about a goal and, thus, also which steps, if any, they take to achieve it. That is why every goal can be as ambitious as it is ambitious, every strategy as well thought out: if the culture does not support both, the project is doomed to failure.

Peter Drucker made his statement with a view to the entire organization. However, the actors involved are usually part of teams, which in turn can have their own (sub)cultures. We therefore focus on **culture at team level**. In particular, we focus on teams in companies. However, our topics are also transferable to teams in, for example, a volunteer or sports environment.

1.1 Why teams often fail

The word *team* is on everyone's lips these days—but few people know the origin of this term. Sure, the word comes from English. But did you know that in the Middle Ages it was used to refer to a large number of draft animals? Back then, *pulling together* was understood to mean something completely different than it does today. In the past, team members were harnessed to the cart and driven by the farmer to maximum power. Fortunately, today's managers are no longer allowed to use a whip—and even if they were, they would hardly reach their goal with it.

Accordingly, the dictionary defines team today as "**a group of people who work together on a task.**" The task determines who is part of the team and how long the team will last. Teams find each other; teams dissolve again; team members change. For while in the Middle Ages, ox and horse could not resist being part of a team, today's teams are based on voluntariness. As a rule, each team member can terminate his or her membership and leave the team at any time.

It is impossible to imagine today's working world without teams. They solve existing problems and develop innovations. According to Professor Rolf van Dick, social psychologist and vice president of the Johann Wolfgang Goethe University Frankfurt am Main, the trend toward teamwork has two reasons. First, technological progress is leading to increasing specialization—in the case of organ transplantation, for example, one surgeon is no longer responsible for the entire operation, but various experts work hand in hand. Second, customers and consumers are demanding new products or solutions to their problems faster than ever before. These expectations can be satisfied only if entire teams are entrusted with the tasks, according to van Dick's thesis (see *WirtschaftsWoche* 48/2017, p. 21).

The dark side of teamwork

But is teamwork always the method of choice? Is teamwork in the end perhaps only a "euphemism of the mediocre for jointly produced average," as the abovementioned article from *WirtschaftsWoche* provocatively asks? Anyone who has ever worked in a team knows that teamwork also has its dark sides: meetings without end, an overflowing email inbox (e.g., because everyone puts everyone else in CC for everything), political games and cat fights among the team members . . . In principle, a group has more potential than an individual to solve a task, but it can also go wrong in the process.

Numerous studies show that **teams are not necessarily more productive and successful**:

- In the nineteenth century, Max Ringelmann discovered that more people does not automatically result in more performance. He had men pull on a rope and measured the force used: if one person pulled alone, he developed a force of 63 kg. Two people together pulled with a force of only 118 kg; that is, 8 kg less than their actual potential. Three people applied a pulling force of 160 kg—29 kg less than possible! This loss of productivity with increased group size is called the **Ringman effect**, which can also be observed in other tasks such as brainstorming. This can be explained by a loss of coordination and motivation. The latter occurs above all when the individual contribution of a person is not recognizable as such, but the person is involved in the overall result of the group (cf. Metz-Göckel 2003, pp. 10–12).

- Benjamin Walker divided 158 students into 33 teams after an individual examination of their conscientiousness. In each team one person had a low sense of duty. Each team was given a set of tasks and the information that they would all receive the same grade depending on their team score. The result was clear: the one person with the low sense of duty pulled down the performance and satisfaction of the whole team. The frustration of having a "free rider" in the team ensured that the others did not try as hard as they could have, so that one person's lack of performance was not compensated for by the rest of the group. Walker's attempt thus underlines the **"one bad apple" theory**—one rotten apple spoils the whole basket (see Burke 2011).

These examples illustrate that teamwork does not necessarily lead to the hoped-for results. There are many other mechanisms and reasons besides the loss of coordination and motivation that cause teams to fail colossally.

Self-reflection
Before you read on, consider the following questions:
- In which teams have I worked for a longer period of time?
- When and for what reasons were we successful as a team?
- When and for what reasons did our team performance fall short of its actual potential?

It is impossible to imagine today's working world, which is characterized by fast pace and specialization, without teams. But working in a team does not always lead to the hoped-for results. Studies have shown that team performance can be significantly smaller in total than the potential of each individual.

1.2 Success through fit

In our experience, teams are most successful when they "fit like a glove": the individual people must fit the group. The group must fit the organization. The organization must fit the market. And the market in turn must fit the individual person.

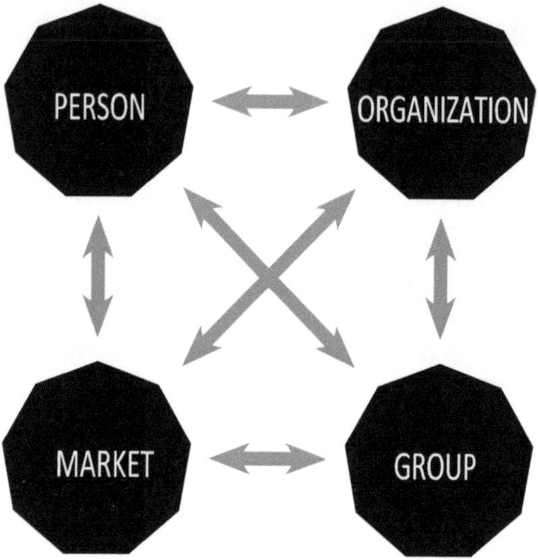

Fig. 1: Interplay of the fit of person, group, organization, and market.

Example: *Imagine a sales team that has been representing its product very successfully in the German market for five years. Now the product is to be transferred to Eastern Europe. The skills of the employees and the motivation of the whole team are consistently high. But regardless of this, the team there cannot build on its old successes in Germany. It lacks the ability to connect to the Eastern European market.*

The innovative work culture of Google is often cited today as a positive example of how teamwork can work. But if such a cocreative, agile team suddenly finds itself in a patriarchal, medium-sized company in a rural area, the team will most likely no longer be successful. But why exactly does this not fit together? How can we make tangible what fits and what doesn't? This requires a closer look at what exactly makes up the culture of teams.

Teams are most successful when the fit of person, organization, group, and market is right. If these four components are in harmony, there is no need for change. However, if only one of these areas changes, an imbalance arises and the other areas are required to adapt accordingly.

1.3 Team culture and the 7-S model

Team culture is comparable to wind: Everyone knows it is there. Everyone feels it. It can feel very light and pleasant, but it can also unleash great destructive power. It is not visible, but only shows itself indirectly through what it does. Nobody doubts its existence—only, we cannot really grasp it.
Accordingly, there is **no clear and generally valid definition of the term team culture**. However, a German industry norm, DIN 69905 on "Project management, terms," dared to define project culture as "the

totality of the behavior of project participants influenced by knowledge, experience and tradition and their general assessment by the project environment." According to this definition, team culture thus appears to be something that, on the one hand, is decisively co-determined by the individuals involved—but is also determined by external factors.
In our search for an approach to comprehensively describe team cultures, we came across the **7-S model developed by management consultants Thomas J. Peters and Robert H. Waterman**. In the 1970s, they and their team asked themselves why organizations are fundamentally very similar in their structure and strategy but have very different success rates. They explained this by the fact that, in addition to **"hard" factors**, such as strategy and structure, there are also **"soft" elements**, such as skills and values, that are critical to success. Although these are more difficult to capture and assess, they are no less important for the overall result.

The seven core variables

In accordance with this finding, Peters and Waterman defined seven core variables that are essential for the design of companies:

- strategy
- structure
- systems
- shared values

- style
- skills
- staff

Together these elements form the *7-S model*, so named because the chosen designations all begin with S.

The 7-S model at team level

We use the 7-S model in a slightly adapted form to describe what makes a team what it is at its core, not at the organizational level, but at the team level:

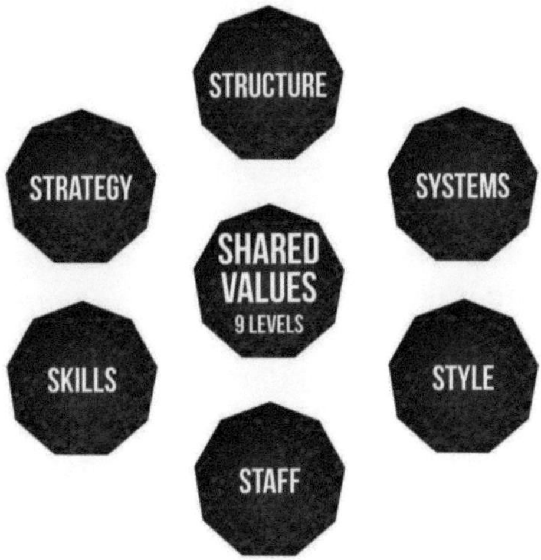

Fig. 2: The seven design elements of team culture. On the outside are the six explicit elements; on the inside is the implicit element, values.

In this context, we describe leadership, employees, skills, processes, structure, and strategy as **explicit design elements of team culture**. They are easy to grasp and often put down in writing; for example, in the context of process descriptions.

Values, however, are an **implicit element of team culture**. They are not directly visible, but only manifest themselves in the design of the explicit elements of team culture. Only through a value analysis—for example, by means of the 9 Levels of Value Systems or value workshops—can they also be made explicit. More on this in chapter 3. In the next chapter we will describe the seven design elements of team culture in detail.

30 ***Team culture is codetermined both by the individuals involved and by external factors. In accordance with the 7-S model from management consultants Thomas J. Peters and Robert H. Waterman, the six explicit design elements (strategy, structure, systems, style, skills, and staff) as well as the implicit design element (values) can be distinguished. Since values are implicit and, thus, unlike the explicit elements and not directly observable, they must be made visible; for example, through value analyses.***

30 MINUTES

How do employees hape the team?

Page 22

To what extent is the team influenced by leadership?

Page 23

Why are values so central to team culture?

Page 33

2. Elements of team culture

Changing team culture sustainably and effectively is difficult. There is always the danger of applying the lever with a lot of effort but in the wrong place. This can be observed in many companies in the context of the current NewWork wave: out of a desire for increased exchange and more agile approaches, conference rooms are being transformed into lounges, and suddenly beanbags are lying around everywhere. But none of this alone will change the team's daily routine! It takes a **holistic view of the various elements of team culture** to actually initiate the desired change and ensure that the changes achieved are maintained in the long term.

On the following pages, we present the explicit and implicit design elements of team culture in detail. They can be used to reflect on the status quo of the team in order to determine later on, in a second step, which of these levers need to be adapted, in which order, and how for sustainable and goal-oriented development.

2.1 Staff

Employees are the most obvious explicit design element of team culture, because only their community makes up an individual part of a group. **Each individual team member shapes the team culture through his or her personality, experience, and knowledge.** To analyze the status quo of a team, the following questions may be relevant:

- How many and which employees does the team have?
- How long have the employees been part of the team?
- What is the professional background of each employee?
- How do the employees' individual competency profiles look in the actual and target situations?
- Which individual values do the employees represent and live?
- Are the results of personality analyses known; for example, on the level of motives or behavior?
- Who takes on which role and responsibility in the team?
- Which private interests and hobbies do the employees have?
- What foreign experience and language skills do the employees have?
- Where in the salary structure are the employees?
- What monetary and nonmonetary incentives do the employees have?

- Which working time measurements do the employees use?
- How satisfied are the employees with their work situation?

Example: *In the management team of a medium-sized family business in a rural area, four out of five members are big football fans. Not only does the team often talk about the sport, but they also gather socially outside of work to watch football games. The fifth team member does not share this passion and often makes it very clear that he or she has neither interest in nor understanding of the others' football enthusiasm. When this person leaves the team, it is clear that the new member should have not only the necessary experience background and competency profile, but also at least a basic interest in football, so that he or she fits well into the team!*

The most obvious design element of team culture is the employees. Each individual team member contributes to the team with his or her personality, experience, and skills and thus shapes the team culture. 30

2.2 Style

If a team leader is present, he or she has a **special role in a team structure: on the one hand, it is as an in-**

tegral part of a team; on the other hand, it stands a little outside.

Whether the team leader sees him- or herself emotionally as part of the team or, rather, as an outsider, and how his or her role and involvement are seen and interpreted by the team members themselves, is quite different. In some teams there is a clear hierarchical difference between leadership and members, with explicitly defined roles and responsibilities. In other groups, the team leadership is only a formality on paper, with little relevance for everyday cooperation, and yet other teams manage completely without classic team leadership. However, these different constellations have one thing in common: they are characteristic of the group's team culture in a very specific way. The following questions can be used to understand and describe leadership as an explicit element of team culture:

- Is there an explicit or implicit leadership role in the team? If so, who carries it out?
- Which responsibilities are associated with the leadership role?
- How is the manager involved in the operational activities of the team?
- What organizational framework and expectations affect the manager?
- What leadership style does the manager practice and how does this manifest itself in everyday team life?
- Which individual values does the manager represent?

- Which leadership style do the team members prefer (e.g., authoritative, participative, goal oriented, . . .)?
- What expectations do the team members have of their leadership?
- Which recognition and sanction mechanisms does the manager have at his or her disposal? Are they used and, if so, how?
- How does the manager deal with his or her own mistakes and those of team members?

Example: *A small consulting firm consists of the owner and two back-office employees. Now an additional back-office employee joins the company, so that the personnel costs increase. The owner asks the employees for suggestions on how further sales could be generated in order to counter-finance the personnel costs. After two weeks they sit down together again and the suggestion is "no suggestion." One wants to continue working as before and not add any new topics or tasks. The owner accepts this, although she would have wished for a different result, and develops her own ideas. The current team culture is very passive and reactive. A boss with different individual values would certainly have acted differently here.*

How a team is managed has a great influence on the respective team culture. In addition to the preferred leadership style, typical communication patterns, unwritten laws, and the handling of mistakes also play a role. 30

2.3 Skills

While the design element *staff* is about the individual competencies of each team member, the **collective capabilities** are highlighted here: What can a team as a whole achieve? In his book *Spuren am Himmel* (*A Trace in the Sky*), world record balloonist Bertrand Piccard describes in a lucid manner that it can be quite different from what the individual skills at team level can accomplish (2003, p. 233ff.):

- **1 + 1 = 2** results when there is little exchange and interaction between team members. Thus, although the people involved are not in competition with each other, no new synergies are developed. Everyone continues to think and do everything as they are used to.
- If the individual team members are also very similar, a relationship formula of **1 + 1 = 1** can even develop, which is very uncreative and lacks innovation.
- **1 + 1 = 0** is possible if power and dominance are major issues in the interaction of the team members.
- When the employees are very different on the one hand, but on the other hand treat each other with great respect and understanding, **1 + 1 = 3** can arise.

Individual abilities are indeed the basis for collective abilities. However, the individual communication and problem solving competencies of the individual employees are not sufficient in themselves to provide comprehensive and outstanding service as a team. How all participants interact and are coordinated is a central element of the team culture. To approach these collective abilities of a team, the following questions may be useful:

- Does the team have the knowledge and experience to successfully achieve its goals?
- What special knowledge does the team have?
- How is knowledge and experience spread and passed on within the team?
- What are the core competencies of the team?
- Which key skills are currently underdeveloped in the team?

Example: *A team of quality assurance experts faces the challenge of allowing more process orientation and co-operation. Individually, each team member has the necessary flexibility and communication skills. However, fears and worries mean that 1 + 1 initially remains 2—after all, the team is also responsible for ensuring that, for example, no small child can choke on a piece of a toy. Only the practice of transparency and cooperation ("Oh, so that's what my colleague does!") leads step by step to the development of comprehensive thinking and 1 + 1 can become the result 3.*

The design element skills is about the question of
what a team as a whole can achieve—and wheth- 30
er the team actually exploits its potential. Com-

munication, dealing with mistakes, and so on determine the overall performance of the individual competencies of the employees.

2.4 Systems

In organizational theory, **process organization** describes all systems and dynamic work processes and refers to space, time, material resources, people, and so on. Analogously, with regard to a team, the design element processes include everything with which a team achieves its **added value**. In other words, it is about the **material and immaterial tools and instruments** that the team uses and follows in everyday life and that set the framework for team productivity:

- At what level of quality, how quickly, and at what cost does the team perform its services?
- What is the team members' workplace arrangement?
- What kind of work equipment is there?
- What budget is available? What rules are there for its use?
- Can the team obtain the information and material resources needed to complete the task?
- How are the inflow and outflow of materials and products handled?
- How are decisions made and actions taken in case of problems?
- How much capacity is being used?

- What are the distribution, throughput, waiting, and idle times?
- What about the adherence to schedules?
- Which IT systems are used?
- Which other services are used to support the work?
- In which degree of maturity is the process pronounced?

Maturity level—what does that mean?
The question of maturity aims to show that different levels of process maturity have a strong influence on how productive the team is and with what quality, in how much time, and at what cost it performs. For example, a process has a very low degree of maturity if it is random and is executed in a different way each time. A moderately mature process, on the other hand, is described basically and is carried out in the same way again and again. A very mature process has great routine. Weaknesses are systematically sought out, and a continuous improvement process is established.

Example: *The design department of a company is being rebuilt because innovations suddenly mean more tasks and more responsibility. Therefore all processes and responsibilities are newly regulated. Among other things, "best practices circles" are being established, and a board with "Hot Shit!" is being opened, where everyone is invited to pin up innovative articles, pictures, and so on and thus make them available to all as a source of inspiration.*

30 *The design element systems includes all tools and instruments with which a team achieves its added value. Different levels of maturity of the processes influence the quality, time, and cost of the team's performance.*

2.5 Structure

While the design element *systems* is based on the process organization of organizational theory, the element *structure* is based on the **organizational plan.** It deals with the **organizational units** of a company and—in this context—with those of a team. At its core is the question of **who gets what information and decisions from whom and passes them on to whom**:

- What connections do the team members have to each other?
- What external connections does the team maintain?
- Which body has what executive authority, authority to issue orders, decision-making authority, authority to have a say, authority to issue directives, authority to represent and control?
- How shielded or interlinked are the individual job profiles?
- Into which subtasks can the overall tasks be divided?

Which structure is the right one?
Which structure is most appropriate in each case depends on the interests of the overall organization, the individual employees, and the customers. In individual cases, these can also differ from and compete with one another. In this case, it must be determined which interest carries what weight.

Example: *A small marketing agency has grown over the years. Originally it was just the two owners, but today it has 15 employees working part and full time. The team maintains a very collegial relationship with each other. They make every effort to ensure that everyone is as well informed as possible about what the other person is doing. However, this increasingly leads to a slowdown in the processing of projects and customer inquiries. Whereas in the past the responsible employee simply made the decision, today he or she often first asks for the opinion of colleagues or is partly responsible for the decision. In the interests of the company and its customers, it was therefore decided to split the entire team into three individual teams that work on and serve their areas and customers largely independently of each other.*

*The structure element considers which organiza-
tional units exist in the team. The question is how* 30
*information can flow and decisions can be made
in the best possible way, taking into account the
interests of the company, individual employees,
and customers.*

2.6 Strategy

By strategy, we understand which **long-term goals or vision** the team is pursuing and which **concrete measures** the team is taking to achieve them:

- What are the vision and mission of the team?
- How are this vision and mission formulated?
- How visible are these in the daily team routine?
- What measures does the team take to fulfil its vision and mission?
- How are these measures formulated?
- How are they tracked?
- What key figures and systems are used to make the status quo and the progress of the achievement of objectives visible?

Example: *At the 9 Levels Institute for Value Systems, our vision is, "We are the leading global institute for scientifically valid measurement of the value systems of individuals, groups, and organizations based on the theory of Clare W. Graves." At an annual team day, we evaluate where we currently stand in relation to this goal and what measures we want to implement in the next 12 months to further contribute to our vision.*

30 *The design element strategy describes which vision and mission a team pursues in the long term and which measures it takes in the short term to approach its goal.*

2.7 Shared Values

Values are an **implicit element** of team culture. They do not manifest themselves directly but **find their expression in the way the explicit elements are formed.**

Values define meaning and significance, provide the foundation for evaluations, and define what is right and what is wrong.

The real values of a team are often not congruent with the values or guidelines laid down by the organization—for example, just think of the large boards with values such as "service orientation" and "innovation" that are often displayed in the lobbies of corporations. Often enough, these values have little to do with the values actually lived by a team. Here we refer to the values that actually significantly shape the way the team members think and act. We also consider the area of conflict that may arise between the values of a team that are predetermined by the organization and those that actually exist:

- Which explicitly formulated values exist within the organization?
- Which values are explicitly formulated at the team level?
- What implicit values of the team can be inferred from the design of the explicit elements?
- To what extent are the organizational values congruent with the explicitly formulated and implicitly existing team values?

Example: *The purchasing team of an Australian retail chain has given itself the following action-guiding values, among others:*

- *Don't leave the kitchen dirty!*
- *If you're not in, you're out!*
- *Don't be No. 5!*
- *Leave a Legacy!*

30 Values are the fundamental element of team culture. They define what the team believes to be right or wrong and thus influence the other design elements—that is, the staff, style, skills, systems, structure, and strategy.

30 MINUTES

How did Clare W. Graves research the development of values?
Page 38

How can value systems be measured?
Page 40

What characterizes teams at the different levels of development?
Page 45

3. Stages of team culture

As discussed in the last chapter, **values are the implicit foundation of any team culture.** They are never right or wrong, but always more or less appropriate to the individual team member, to the organization surrounding the team, and to the market in which the team operates. **Values are dynamic.** Influences from outside or inside can lead to pressure for change, resulting in a shift in values.

Through his research, **Clare W. Graves** has been able to show that there are specific patterns of how value systems develop from such internal or external pressures for change. **Value systems—and thus also team culture—change gradually.** Just as a small child must first learn to crawl before he or she can stand up and walk, value development follows a specific pattern. In this chapter, we describe the individual stages of value development. We describe which values are in the foreground at each stage and how they manifest themselves in the everyday life of the team with regard to the explicit elements of team culture.

3.1 The Graves model

Clare W. Graves (1914–1986) was a professor of psychology at Union College in New York (United States). He was active not only in research but also as a consultant for many years. A central aim of his research was to elucidate the developmental stages of the human being. When he gave his students the task of writing a report in which they were to describe "the adult human being," recurring elements came to his attention during the analysis of the results: the **different developmental stages of human existence**. Graves first published the results of this research from the 1950s in a 1966 *Harvard Business Review* article entitled "Deterioration of Work Standards." In this article he referred to his model as "Levels of Human Behavior." Later he called his theory an "**emergent, cyclical double-helix model of adult biopsychosocial systems development**." This means it is an upwardly striving, cyclical double helix of adult human development and its biopsychosocial system.

The Graves model is thus an approach that describes the diversity of human development not only in a very complex way but also in a multiperspective way. Graves combined elements from four different scientific disciplines in his approach—biology/neurobiology, psychology/personality type theory, sociology/anthropology, and systems theory.

After Graves's death, his former students **Christopher Cowan and Don Beck** published his model for the first time under the name **Spiral Dynamics**, which is how it is now known and recognized worldwide. They also designated colors for the different development stages. In the meantime, many books have been published presenting different applications of the basic Graves model. Because the Graves value system depicts how individuals or entire systems, such as teams, companies, or organizations, think and act, it is a useful tool for all those who work in or with teams or organizations and want to understand them better. Nevertheless, the Graves model remains a theoretical science model in itself. For Rainer Krumm, the logical consequence of this was the further development of the model into a valid scientific analysis model: the **9 Levels of Value Systems.**

30 *The Graves model describes the successive stages of value development for humans. Later, Rainer Krumm developed the Graves model into a valid scientific analysis model, the 9 Levels of Value Systems.*

3.2 The 9 Levels of Value Systems

The 9 Levels of Value Systems is a simplification of Graves's theory and makes the **value development of people, groups, and organizations** measurable. Because when it comes to implicit factors like values, leaders and managers are looking for something they can grasp. They like to orient themselves on numbers, because numbers give them the security they need for projects, for decisions, and in relation to employees and superiors.

Using **scientifically valid analysis sheets**, the 9 Levels of Value Systems surveys the current status quo and/or the target status of the value systems of a person, group, or organization. The model records how pronounced the respective level is. On the other hand, it also illuminates whether there is resistance to the respective level and how strong that resistance is; that is, to what extent the person, group, or organization does not agree with the values and the thought and behavior patterns derived from them.

Personal Value System

The **Personal Value System** is the analysis sheet of the 9 Levels of Value Systems that deals with the **value system of an individual person—focused on one area of life**.

As the sample evaluation diagram shows, it is less about a single level (section 3.3 explains which concrete values characterize a level) but rather about the interaction of all levels. Some values are particularly relevant in the current phase of life and in the respective context, such that the corresponding level is currently at its highest level. Other values were once particularly relevant but were then replaced by new val-

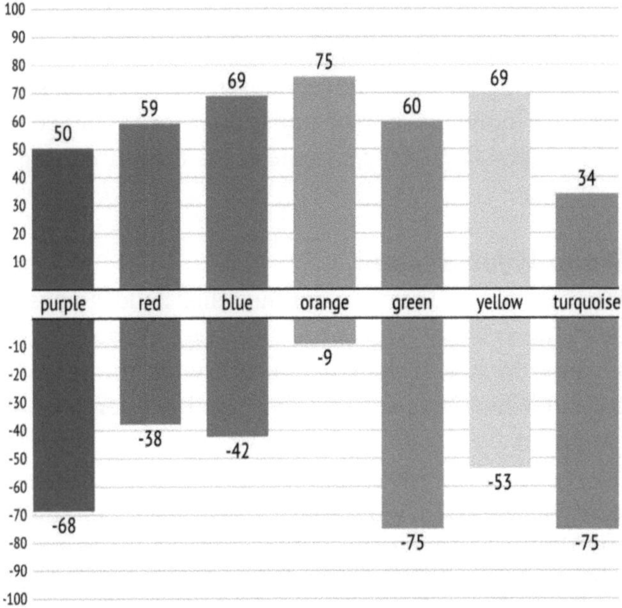

Fig. 3: Example of a Personal Value System. The person has the highest level at orange and the strongest resistance at the green and turquoise levels.

ues—these are (often, but not always) the values that are to the left of the current highest level in the evaluation graphic. They do not simply disappear but are integrated into the current value dynamics and continue to be effective. Still other values have the potential to be of particular relevance to us one day. However, they are still foreign to us and only partially anchored in our current value system. As a rule, these are located in the evaluation chart to the right of the current highest level. The Personal Value System describes the value system of an individual person and is therefore assigned to the category *staff* in the scheme of team culture design elements.

Group Value System

The **Group Value System**, on the other hand, analyses the **value system of a group from the perspective of the individuals**. It does not record what the team is like but which values the team members perceive at team level.

The results can be very similar to the results of the Personal Value System—but they can also be quite different. Although meaningful hypotheses about the entire team can be derived from the average of all team members' Personal Value Systems, the Group Value System enables further, literally valuable, insights into the design element *values*.

Perception of the team culture

Experience shows that teams whose members have a very similar perception of their team values (Group Value System) are more successful/compatible. Even in such a case, the individual value systems of the team members can be very different. The only decisive factor is the same perspective on the team's value system.

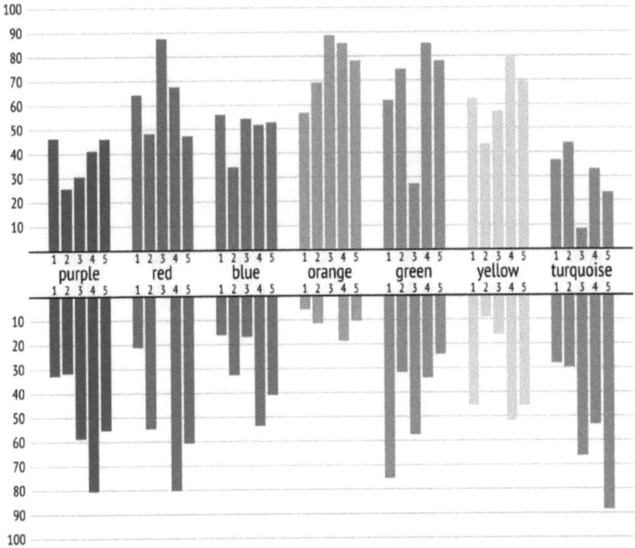

Fig. 4: Example of a Group Value System of a team with five members. The first bar of each level is from the person whose Personal Value System is shown in Fig. 3—there are clear differences between PVS and GVS. While, for example, level red is only partially relevant for the person himself (see Fig. 3), he perceives the level in the team most strongly. While he personally shows a high resistance to level turquoise, this resistance is only slightly pronounced at team level.

Using the 9 levels

Access to the scientific analyses via a Personal Value System and/or Group Value System is provided by a certified 9 levels consultant. But already your basic knowledge of the Graves model and a more detailed knowledge of the individual levels will enable you to **draw conclusions about the implicit values of a team from the explicit design elements.** You can then move on to consciously shaping team culture, either by specifically adapting the explicit design elements to generate pressure for change in the implicit values or by carrying out value-based interventions of a cross-value nature (see chapter 4).

30 *The 9 Levels of Value Systems is a further development and simplification of the Graves model. Using scientifically valid analysis sheets, it makes the value systems of individuals, groups, and organizations measurable and visible.*

3.3 Levels and team culture

In the following we would like to introduce the **levels purple, red, blue, orange, green, yellow, and turquoise** and their concrete manifestation on the levels of style, staff, skills, systems, structure, and strategy. Please note that in our explanations we deal with only the levels that are relevant to the topic of team culture. For this reason, we will leave the first level, beige, and the last level, coral, out of our considerations. These two levels are not measured even in a 9-level analysis.

What about beige and coral?
Beige is all about values at the level of basic needs. A group in beige is a small, loose association that has no organizational structures but serves only for survival and reproduction.
The ninth level, coral, is only rudimentarily described so far. It is already intimated, but there are not many individuals, let alone teams, in coral. Probably coral will be about values like courage and strength—but not on a self-centered, individual level; rather, with focus on and respect for all living beings.

Please also note that in the following we present the levels individually and in pure form for clarification. As the sample evaluation graphics of the Personal Value System and Group Value System illustrate, in reality no person, team, or organization has a value system that is anchored only at one level. It is always a **mix of current and previous values as well as values that are already foreseeable but not yet integrated.** So imagine the value systems like the dimmer of a light switch; you can have a light of varying brightness on several levels in a house, and the same is true for the model. If you go to the next level, the previous values are usually reduced a little and then the new values are turned up accordingly on the current level.

Purple

The purple level is basically about **belonging to a community, clan, tribe, group—with a patriarch or ma-**

triarch, a chief, or a leader. The highest priority is to ensure the existence and survival of this group. Management and colleagues expect from the employees 100 percent loyalty to the team and to the overall organization, right up to sacrifice. The willingness to do so is created by a high emotional bond between the team member and the company. The members of a team proudly distinguish themselves from other teams by individual signs, just as the knight clans once did in the Middle Ages.

> **Central values of purple:** tradition, kinship, customs, home, rituals, obedience, protection, willingness to sacrifice, commitment, belonging

The values of purple are reflected in the explicit elements of team culture as follows:

Staff: Employees identify strongly with the team and work long and hard when properly managed. They care for each other and often show symbols of their affiliation; for example, by wearing team shirts and jackets. Belonging is understood in the sense of "all or nothing at all"—someone belongs either fully or not at all. A new team member can easily weaken the whole group, because they tend to become isolated rather than integrated. The employees do not like competition. They see power and decision-making authority lying clearly with their supervisor. They carry out simple tasks that are very similar and never so complex that no one else could do them as well. Men and women occupy predominantly traditional roles. There are no clearly defined development processes for the individual. There are also no clearly defined models for working hours, salary, and so on—every employee works to the extent and receives the remuneration for this work that is determined by the superior or head of the company.

Style: The team is usually led centrally by the supervisor. He or she is responsible for all decision-making processes. He or she is the focal point and leads the team in a friendly and benevolent, but very close and direct, manner, which also corresponds to the preferences of the employees. They find it inappropriate if they are too involved and the superior delegates too much responsibility. Accordingly, it is the supervisor who determines who in the team takes on which task and how this is compensated for. His or her decisions are characterized by strong communication: everyone has the right to express their opinions and share them with everyone else. But the superior then forms the consensus that everyone follows. Status symbols are exclusively for the superior; his or her position and status are not questioned. In return, the employees expect him or her to provide security and safeguard their basic needs. This, in turn, is taken for granted.

Skills: The main competency of the team lies in the good and routine execution of the few tasks and processes that it has been assigned by the organization.

Systems: Work is mainly carried out according to the instructions of the superior, and these are not questioned. The (less complex) core processes are clearly structured and defined and are carried out step by step and always in the same way.
Structure: The structure is basically two tiered. There is a manager at the top and the employees "below." Although there are formally no other hierarchical levels, the employees do not stand on one level but are arranged in a fixed order of precedence according to the subjective preference of the superior.
Strategy: The strategy of the team is strongly influenced by the supervisor and is primarily designed to maintain the status quo. It is not formulated nor are there defined measures for its implementation.

Red

For a red team, **power** and the unconditional **preservation of its own independence** are central.

> **Central values of red:** power, courage, strength, dominance, honor, aggression, winning at all costs, reputation, avoidance of "shame," personal success

The ego plays a much greater role on the red level than the "we." Therefore red teams are often rather **unstable.** As soon as the individual believes that he or she can achieve his or her goals faster and more successfully without the group, he or she leaves it. Especially in situations where the members are supposed to support and strengthen each other, it becomes clear that red teams are on shaky ground. Yet, red groups can develop an **enormous power of impact**, because they quickly take the initiative, act powerfully, and focus everything on their success.

The core values of red often show up as follows in the explicit elements of team culture:

Staff: The team consists of a broad mass of interchangeable employees who perform the same or very similar activities—they are like speedboats racing more or less coordinated toward the more or less same goal. New employees are trained. However, once they are involved in their tasks, no further qualification takes place. All employees know exactly what has to be done and what the result should look like. Therefore, they want a certain amount of freedom for decisions. They are proud of their skills and expect respect and rewards for good and quickly completed jobs. For the individual employee, however, belonging to the team is above all a means to an end, to secure and increase his or her own well-being. Therefore, remuneration is mainly based on individual performance. Exceptionally good performance is rewarded with high incentives. As a result, power struggles and competition occur again and again, with no consideration for the opponent. The manager even instigates these fights. In addition to financial rewards, employees draw much of their motivation from respect for the successful leader, to whom they direct all their actions.

Style: Typical for red team cultures is an autocratic and authoritarian leadership style. Decisions are made from top to bottom. Since mistakes are unconditionally punished, employees do everything to avoid or cover up failures and thus "shame." Communication to give instructions takes place from top to bottom, whereas for reporting purposes it is from bottom to top. The style of communication is characterized by the pursuit and retention of power, so that propagandistic speeches and censorship by superiors can occur. Also, no employee receives a comprehensive overview of what is happening—because knowledge is power. The leader makes him- or herself indispensable, and almost everything is a "matter for the boss." At the same time, practically anyone can become the boss if they have sharp elbows. Even the leader once fought hard for his or her position and must defend it again and again. On the one hand, they have to prove that none of the employees can do the job better than they themselves do, and on the other hand, they have to constantly create incentives to ensure that the employees put their best foot forward.

Skills: A red team is fast, powerful, and assertive. The team members do their utmost to achieve their goals—without regard to losses.

Systems: The little-defined routine processes are described and are always executed in the same way. There are no planning and managing tools yet. IT support is also rudimentary. Resources are mainly distributed according to power: whoever is more powerful will prevail.

Structure: The team is characterized by a strict hierarchy that separates superiors from employees and does not further subdivide them functionally. A classic red team comprises six to 15 employees.

Strategy: In a red group construct, there is no formulated vision or strategy. The rule is the more, the better—no matter which way. Objectives are neither long term nor sustainable. The focus is on short-term success, quick returns, and power (gains).

Blue

Blue teams are usually large groups that are strongly subdivided within themselves. There are **clear structures and responsibilities according to which people live and act.** Procedures are firmly prescribed and documented. No one has special rights; everyone must adhere to **universal rights and duties.** Each team member has his or her "rank," within which he or she can move and make decisions in order to fulfil his or her tasks and responsibilities. However, everything must be done correctly—the given laws and regulations must always be observed. The common blue values weld the members firmly together.

> **Central values of blue:** quality, discipline, loyalty, order, reliability, safety, duty, stability, truth, patience

The values of the blue level are often reflected in the team culture as follows:

Staff: The employees naturally perform their work well and conscientiously, and they often have a professional specialization. They reliably carry out the tasks assigned to them and make the necessary decisions within a defined scope of responsibility. They try to avoid mistakes and guilt. They expect recognition for their performance; for example, in the form of certificates and diplomas. They also want job security and a continuous increase in wages. They see this as a sign of loyalty and pay this back with many years of work and even lifelong loyalty (often over several generations). For them, titles and ranks as well as the corresponding status symbols play a major role—in the blue world, it is simply a matter of fact that a promotion, for example, also means a massive change in the office furnishings, from birch to precious wood. Promotions, as well as the basic salary level, are primarily based on formal criteria (such as years of service) and not on individual performance. There are numerous instructions for conduct, user manuals, and quality standards for the performance of activities. Clearly defined areas of competency are welcomed by the employees. Their working hours are clearly regulated and uniform. Key figures are available to them in very detailed form, but employees find it difficult to aggregate them and derive correlations from them. In principle, they accept their supervisor because of his or her position and hierarchical level.

Style: An authoritarian and correspondingly directive management style with strictly hierarchical communication prevails. The leaders represent the team, create a framework of order, and facilitate routine. They structure tasks and define and clarify rules. They do not wish or expect the employees to think and act beyond the framework assigned to them. A lack of leadership and of clear direction is perceived by the team as demotivating and inappropriate. The team also interprets a cooperative leadership style or an openness to discussion as a sign of weakness on the part of the superior.
Skills: The main skill of a blue team is to follow rules and work within the given framework. "Better slow than wrong" is one of the central maxims of action, which often shows itself in 120 percent results.
Systems: All work processes are clearly regulated and described. The procedure is often highly fragmented and is not linked to the value chain of the subsupplier. Planning and managing processes are described and implemented at a low level of maturity. However, they do not go beyond the boundaries of individual areas but remain within the framework of their own unit. Many IT systems are used.
Structure: A strictly hierarchical structure ensures clarity and equity. The team is functionally organized with clear responsibilities.
Strategy: There is often a strategy formulated by the supervisor that aims to ensure the existence and size of the team. Employees are not involved in the formula-

tion and design of the strategy. However, there are often no uniform mechanisms for developing the measures needed to actually implement the strategy.

Orange

With an orange team culture, the **success of the team** is the focus of attention. Each individual feels responsible for the performance of the group and does everything to move the team forward.

> **Central values of orange:** performance, responsibility, status/status symbols, competition, productivity, process, result and profit orientation, entrepreneurial thinking, value creation

Orange teams **do not want to be slowed down unnecessarily by restrictive measures**. Orange teams do not even have complicated structures, because they take up valuable time. Although there are rules and regulations, they always contribute directly to the result (unlike blue). If any process does not run smoothly, leaner procedures are immediately sought in order to become more capable of action again. This can be seen in the explicit elements of an orange team culture as follows:

Staff: Members of an orange team have a lot of responsibility and are very aware of it. They want to contribute individually and proactively. They strive for the success of the team because it is also worthwhile for them personally. Customer and market orientation is firmly anchored in their thinking. They want to get involved so that the team has maximum success—and be the best at it. This competitive thinking drives the team members to top performance and motivates them even more. Nevertheless, the other members should not be harmed on the way to the goal. On the contrary, the ambition of the individual also benefits all others in the community, because after all, the whole team always benefits from the individual commitment of its members. Those who are not the best themselves can still boast of belonging on the orange level—because success is achieved by those who work for a successful company. In addition, the individual does not need to fear that there are others who do a good job. The important thing is that this does not diminish one's own success. Accordingly, the employee expects to be rewarded for his or her work and commitment. Rewards or incentives are in demand to show off one's own success. Salary development and promotions are based on the measurable employee goals that are usually set annually. Employees are expected to think and act entrepreneurially. Every employee has access to the necessary information at all times. Working hours are flexible. Key figures are of great importance, as they can be used to measure and visualize success or failure.

Style: In an orange team culture, you will usually find a competitive leadership style. The leader controls and leads on the basis of goals. Managers use clear reward and sanction systems. They delegate a lot and give employees extensive and complex tasks with a great deal of freedom to make decisions, because they know that they can fully rely on their people. Communication is very open and also works across departments.

Skills: A core competency of an orange team is to react quickly and flexibly to challenges. An orange team looks beyond the horizon so that there is planning across areas of responsibility. Clear priorities are adhered to.

Systems: An orange team is very process oriented. Efficiency and effectiveness are desired, so that key figures of the process are defined and measured. Existing processes are continuously optimized. They all have a high degree of maturity and are massively supported by IT (for example, ERP systems).

Structure: The structure of the team is flat, lean, and procedural. There are few administrative roles and tasks. Individual areas of responsibility predominantly comprise complete processes of the value chain. The various areas of responsibility are strongly interlinked. Temporary project teams are created and dissolve again when they are no longer considered useful.

Strategy: An orange team culture is characterized by the pursuit of success, which is usually understood to mean an increase in sales or a reduction in costs. Strategy is of central importance for this. It is created, filled with life, and implemented with the participation of the employees.

Green

Like all other levels, green is a counterreaction to the previous level—in this case the predominantly egocentric orange. **In green teams the "we" is in the foreground.** Therefore green teams are characterized by tolerance, mutual appreciation, and acceptance. Conflicts hardly play a role; **harmony** is a key concept. Should differences of opinion arise, all parties involved are listened to in order to find a common solution. If a success becomes apparent, it is not seen as a short-term achievement from the here and now, but as the result of a functioning team. This strengthens the cohesion, which is perceived as absolutely beneficial.

> **Central values of green:** cooperation, tolerance, consensus, dialogue, empathy, participation, equality, appreciation, fairness, harmony

The diversity of the team members is strongly supported in order to have as many skills as possible available. Each group member represents a personality that is important for the functioning of the team. Each member is taken seriously and accepted. If someone new joins the team, they are warmly welcomed and quickly integrated. If the team as a whole functions optimally, it is also completely OK if the individual takes a step back—the main thing is that the well-being of the community does not suffer. The cohesion within the team is additionally supported by **joint undertakings**.

Accordingly, the explicit elements of a green team culture are often designed in this way:

Staff: The team members are the core resource of a green team, which is characterized by its heterogeneous composition. The different skills and qualifications of the individuals are understood and used as resources available to all. The employees appreciate the cooperation. They develop and decide together, because they believe that they can be most successful if everyone pulls together. The credo is "Together we can achieve more than each of us individually." This can lead to an individual exhausting him- or herself out of the desire for acceptance and appreciation and overestimating his or her powers—there is a certain danger of burnout if someone wants to be accepted and belong. On the other hand, the group is quite tolerant of an individual's weaknesses, at least to a certain extent. Mistakes are seen as natural; they happen and can be learned from and consequences drawn. However, if they occur more frequently, remedial action is taken quickly and a solution is sought in the interest of all. All in all, the motivation of the employees functions via a community-oriented sense of purpose and joint, long-term success. Decisions are made by consensus. Instead of financial compensation and status symbols, the individual is interested in an expression of appreciation for his or her commitment. Since the focus is shifting away from individual and toward joint performance, team bonuses are awarded rather than individual incentives. The salary structure is very homogeneous, understandable for everyone, and often transparent for all. Working hours are not necessarily fixed. But since life balance is an important issue, the hours must be socially acceptable and can vary according to the phase of life—from flexible part-time to work-anywhere models.

Style: The leadership style in a green team culture is open, participative, and cooperative. Group processes are actively managed without patronizing. Communication is appreciative and clear. Information is an essential asset and is understood and lived as an obligation to provide. The manager is also a team member and must be able to "endure" that his or her proposals are discussed and put to the test in the team. The great challenge for a manager in a green team environment is to meet the group at eye level on the one hand and not to be completely equal to the group on the other. If the leadership style becomes too loose, an unintended momentum could develop. However, if the manager tries too clearly to assert him- or herself, strong resistance arises.

Skills: Green teams use individual skills in a cooperative sense and can actually turn 1+1 into 3. They know how to deal with different competencies; learn from experience, exchange, and reflection; and continuously improve.

Systems: The planning, control, and value-creation processes are very mature and highly collaborative so that everyone can give their best for the common goals. Governance processes are typical because of the special importance of the employees.

Structure: Green teams are often embedded in matrix structures with multiple reporting lines. The teams themselves have a flexible structure and, depending on the task, repeatedly form subteams and project teams, some of which exist parallel to each other and dissolve when their task is completed.

Strategy: Even on the green level, there is a striving for success in terms of increasing sales and reducing costs. In contrast to orange, however, there is a stronger human component. It is not only about monetary success, but sustainable goals at the employee level are also collectively determined and formulated.

Yellow

The levels we have described so far all fall under the term "first-rank level." They react mainly to what happens in the immediate living world. One does not yet think about things from a metaperspective, and acts accordingly.

This changes from the yellow level onward. **Yellow is the first level of the second rank**, on which the levels are repeated on a higher level. The focus is no longer on the immediate being, as in beige, but on a higher sense. While beige focused on issues of physical survival, the values of yellow focus on spiritual issues; that is, on **meaningfulness and the need for meaning.**

> **Central values of yellow:** self-reflection, multiperspectivity, knowledge, creativity, networking, autonomy, individuality, personal responsibility, personal development, profound competence

The core of yellow team cultures is therefore about **permanent learning, knowledge increase, and further development**. Material successes and rewards, power, and status have little relevance.

It is questionable whether a mature yellow can still be called a team at all—because **yellow values and goals are often in general contradiction with a classic team construct**. Nevertheless, in order to provide a better overview and comparability, we have tried to describe a yellow team culture using the previous scheme of explicit design elements:

Staff: While the employees of green teams draw strong motivation from their fixed team membership, the employees of yellow teams see the group primarily as a means to an end. It is useful, but from the beginning it is seen as a temporary structure with a certain finiteness. The individual is a member as long as he or she considers his or her participation as meaningful. Often, membership is not exclusive either: the members act in different teams at the same time—it is rather a network-like structure than a team in the classical sense. If differences of opinion arise, they are openly communicated and dealt with within the team. Concealments or cover-ups do not occur. The members love their freedom and do not want to be restricted in their independence. They are not "manageable" in the classical sense and only accept goal-oriented guidelines. A leader is not accepted per se, but high quality and quantity requirements are set for the employees. Employees want to have an open relationship with the manager and let him or her know what is needed to fulfil their tasks. In addition, they expect to be given a platform for top performance, to be able to act with a high degree of self-control, and to not be subject to any restrictions. This also includes working hours: they are as flexible as possible. Everyone can decide for themselves when and where and how they want to work.

Style: A yellow leadership is above all a supportive one. Innovative strength, flexibility, knowledge, and competence are seen and encouraged. Open communication and especially the exchange of knowledge are very important. All topics are discussed together, from the task definition to the achievement of objectives. It is desired and expected of the manager that he or she do everything possible so that the employees can fully develop and work for the team—especially if creative communication models and working models have to be developed and made possible for this purpose. A manager who did not take responsibility for achieving the team goals and did not support the employees professionally and personally would not be accepted.

Skills: Yellow teams are excellent at the highly flexible use of networks and thinking in large contexts. They think and act systemically and with a great capacity for abstraction. Another important competency is the capacity for multiperspectivity: for the first time, yellow teams are able to recognize, use, and combine the advantages of the previous levels in order to ideally achieve their own goal. Team members are able not only to put themselves in the position of another person but also to think and act from this perspective.

Systems: In a yellow team culture, processes are very mature and are subject to constant optimization so that they can be adapted quickly and flexibly to current situations. The use of information systems is very important. Collaboration systems, communication systems, and knowledge management systems predominate. There is also a great focus on governance processes and the establishment and expansion of regulations and structures so that all available resources can be used with maximum added value.

Structure: A yellow team usually has no fixed structure. Instead, depending on what is considered appropriate for the situation, hierarchical and nonhierarchical structures are created by very different forms of learning and working. The team is a network of individuals who temporarily form a group. This network couples with the different working models of the other levels of the Graves value system or creates them specifically. Hierarchies play no real role. Once established, the structures are only of short duration and can be completely rebuilt with the next task.

Strategy: Because the yellow team is travelling in loose networks, it can be controlled only by clear objectives and predefined rules. The team either sets its own goals—depending on how it is put together—or is given them. Once the goal has been defined, the team of individuals, and in some cases, of other teams, is assembled in the way that is best for achieving the goal. Often, however, it is more important for the team to try something completely new and broaden its horizons than to achieve key figures. Success is primarily defined intellectually and meaningfully, not monetarily.

Turquoise

The level turquoise has only recently emerged. In our opinion, **hardly any team cultures are actually predominantly turquoise—if they exist at all.**

The values that are at the heart of turquoise are very abstract and for many people hardly tangible. Language follows reality—we have not yet found the right words to express what turquoise is all about.

> **Central values of turquoise:** sustainability, holon (whole as part of another whole), responsibility for the future of life, acceptance of global complexity, collective intuition, spiritual awareness, global reconciliation, high ideals, networking, farsightedness

From our point of view, with turquoise, it is therefore even more questionable than with yellow whether it is even possible to speak of what we classically refer to as "team." To some extent, the explicit design elements can be summarized in this way:

Staff: The members of the team focus on the welfare of the world and orient their lives and work accordingly. Everything is judged on whether or not suffering is inflicted upon this holon. The only thing that matters is the overall long-term benefit to all.

Style: The team acts intuitively, always keeping the big picture in mind. It no longer needs guidance in the classical sense.

Skills: Turquoise thinks holistically/globally, ecologically, and intuitively. A turquoise team manages to hold together many different levels with good energy and to unite them toward a global goal.

Systems: A turquoise team stands above processes and tools in the modern sense. The rules are implicit but a matter of course and do not need to be followed.

Structure: The group sees itself as a truly holistic construct. It does not form a solid and impenetrable unit but is permeable and easily integrates other groups and individuals.

Strategy: Turquoise teams are committed to a high ethical value. The ability to act and the understanding of self-responsibility available on the yellow level is placed here in a larger, all-encompassing context. Each goal must be placed in a social and ecological setting of meaning and overall context.

30 *The individual levels shape the explicit design elements of team culture as follows:*

- *Purple: Values such as tradition, obedience, and commitment are reflected in the exclusive decision-making power of the superior, a two-tiered structure, and less complex processes.*
- *Red: Values such as power, courage, and strength are manifested by authoritarian leadership, penetrating power (ability), and competition among employees.*
- *Blue: Values such as quality, discipline, and loyalty are reflected in dutiful employees, a strictly hierarchical structure, and clearly regulated processes.*
- *Orange: Values such as performance, productivity, and goal orientation lead to competition among employees; a flat, process-based structure; and continuous process optimization.*
- *Green: Values such as cooperation, appreciation, and community are reflected in the rapid integration of new members, cooperative leadership, and the pursuit of "soft" factors such as employee satisfaction.*
- *Yellow: Values such as multiperspectivity, independence, and further development mean that the group is structured as a loose network rather than a classic team.*
- *Turquoise: For the central values such as sustainability, collective intuition, and global rec-*

onciliation, an adequate design of the explicit elements still has to be developed—if this is necessary at all.

30 MINUTES

Why is resistance also a good sign?

Page 72

In what directions can team culture be changed?

Page 73

What are the value-based forms of intervention?

Page 82

4. Development of team culture

There is no such thing as one true team culture. As already explained, it always depends on the fit of the group with the team members, the organization, and the market. Because our world is VUCA, a team culture also has to adapt again and again. VUCA is an acronym for the terms *volatility*, *uncertainty*, *complexity*, and *ambiguity* and is currently on everyone's lips when it comes to the framework conditions of our present time. This **continuous adaptation of team culture** to its changing environment occurs automatically; for example, in response to a change of team members, new guidelines from the umbrella organization, or new competitors in the market. A development of the team culture can also be initiated and controlled quite consciously. If, for example, customer needs change, a quick reaction is needed to keep the team at the forefront. This is where the explicit elements of team culture come into play. They are the **set screws with which pressure for change is generated, and an adjustment can be initiated and developed quite consciously.**

4.1 Resistance to change

Every change means that the familiar and proven must be abandoned. It is **therefore** understandable that **development does not take place without fear and resistance**—after all, nobody can foresee what the future will bring and whether the changes will actually lead to improvements.

It is not important what changes. It is enough to change something to arouse skepticism, fear, and resistance. Such resistance is often seen as negative and destructive. For a successful transformation, however, it is crucial to **accept resistance and work with it, not against it**. Resistance can fulfil an important protective function, shielding team members from being overwhelmed and from seemingly nonsensical or harmful changes. At the same time, resistance is a good sign, as it signals interest and concern for the people involved. Successful development of a team culture therefore requires the productive integration of resistance into the change process. If the explicit design elements are transformed in order to generate pressure for change at the value level, the team must be prepared to make adjustments with a certain degree of willingness and openness. Otherwise, it is imperative to first analyze the causes of the resistance and to redesign the measures in such a way that the team is prepared to cooperate in the direction of the change and not to revolt.

Changes are usually associated with resistance. The successful development of team culture requires recognizing resistance and incorporating it productively into the change process through appropriate measures. 30

4.2 Directions of change

Change in team culture can basically take place in three different ways: **on one level, downward, and upward.**

The classic form of cultural development takes place within a level. For this purpose, the existing explicit elements of team culture are stabilized and expanded to match the implicit values.

Example: *In a strongly orange sales team, a new commission model is introduced that, in line with orange values, such as performance, responsibility, and results orientation, enlarges the monetary rewards for individuals' positive results and increases competition between employees.*

A downward change may be necessary if a team has massive problems and cannot stabilize at the current level. In this case, you go back one level in the design of the explicit elements to strengthen old values.

Example: *In a strongly orange sales team, there is a lot of travel. Since a pleasant trip and high-quality accommodations are considered compensation for effort or in-*

centive for performance, the team members book according to comfort and prestige maximization and not necessarily according to business considerations. In order to contain the escalating travel costs and to strengthen blue values such as discipline and duty, the processes surrounding travel booking are defined more closely and more clearly.

A third option is a change upward. It may be appropriate to consider the next level when the organization or the market "pushes" the team's value development upward.

Example: *In a strongly orange sales team, people tend to work side by side rather than together. The employees are primarily focused on achieving their personal goals. However, increasing market integration requires a more intensive exchange between employees. In order to promote green values such as dialogue and community, collaborative elements are integrated into individual target agreements.*

Transformations to a higher level are the most common reason for team development. We focus on three developmental directions that are currently under the greatest strain: **from blue to orange, from orange to green, and from green to yellow.**

There's no elevator!
No level can be skipped. A direct transformation, for example from blue to green, is not possible: a team must first learn to perform on and appreciate the individual level before real collaboration can develop.

From blue to orange

In teams with a strong blue culture, implicit values such as quality, order, reliability, safety, and duty shape the explicit design characteristics. There are clear areas of responsibility and tasks; the procedures are prescribed. There are no special rights of any kind, only universal rights and duties for all team members. Everyone has fixed boundaries within which they can make decisions and ensure that all tasks are carried out reliably in compliance with the regulations. It is important for the team that everything is done correctly.

A pressure to change toward orange arises when the blue team culture no longer matches the team members, the organization surrounding the group, and/or the market.

Example: *A team of engineers has an extremely high level of expertise. Even if they sometimes take longer, their developments are always of high quality. Now, however, the market is changing—massive cost pressure is occurring. Faster, much more dynamic processes are required. Currently, issues are often being addressed that are technically correct and important but which do not add value for the customer. Now the team must establish a much stronger customer orientation.*

A team arrested in blue is struggling with such demands from the orange world. **Instead of being successful through the strengths of blue, blue now stands in the way of success** through slow decisions, rigidity, inflexibility, and black-and-white thinking and acting. A blue team is used to managing—but is now supposed to design. Proactivity should replace reactivity. The team should break away from its routines and structures and favor thinking and acting in an innovative and entrepreneurial way. Suddenly, the focus is no longer on the function of the team, but on the performance of each individual.

Interventions at the level of explicit elements can accelerate the transformation of a blue to an orange team culture. We call one measure for this "**scarifying processes.**" In horticulture, a scarifier is used to remove cuttings and moss so that the soil is better aerated and the lawn can grow better.

Analogously, we support the team in a workshop to **question** their **established procedures, processes, rules, and structures**: What is still valid? What is outdated? If the team can free itself from procedural burdens, it can act more flexibly and clearly and prepare itself for orange challenges.

Example: *After one of these workshops, the management team of a mechanical engineering company in Bavaria committed itself to review 80 percent of its processes each year and to adjust 20 percent of them. In the past, the company's internal travel expense guidelines were a very complex set of rules—it was precisely defined which hotel could be booked by whom, how, at what price, and so on. Based on the premise "Act as if it were your own company," there is now much more self-responsibility and only rough framework regulations with pos-*

sible exceptions: if you now want to book a hotel that is more expensive than usual but does not require a taxi, you can do this in an uncomplicated way!

From orange to green

Characteristic values of an orange team culture are performance, prestige in the sense of status symbols, career orientation, goal orientation, productivity, competition, entrepreneurial thinking, value creation, and innovation. This can be seen in the fact that each individual assumes a great deal of responsibility. Compared to blue, there are few clear rules and fixed structures, because the team does not want to slow down unnecessarily. Less is more here—after all, the result should be outstanding. If a process flow is slowed down by something, the team looks for leaner processes that will restore the desired speed and flexibility.

Orange is effective and productive. But the team members, the surrounding organization, and/or the market can evolve, the fit of the team culture can become no longer a given, and a **pressure for change toward green** can arise.

Example: *The international sales team of a specialized pharmaceutical company serves only a few customers and instead handles very extensive and long-term projects. Each team member has individual goals, the achievement of which is linked to large bonus payments. However, it is increasingly difficult to achieve these goals alone because the complexity of projects is intensifying. If you look at only* *your own sales territory, you will lack knowledge about the laboratories in other countries, for example. Only through real cooperation can the individual sales targets be achieved—but this, however, has so far only been anchored in the team culture to a limited extent.*

The dark sides of orange are greed, strong competition, and high pressure to perform. **The objectively measurable result is in the foreground, not the subjective well-being of the individual.** Team members in an orange team are classic burnout candidates. In order not to burn out, it is suddenly a matter of shifting down a gear. Success is still the top priority but should no longer be achieved at the expense of the individual. There is a desire for more togetherness and a social system characterized by acceptance and appreciation.

To illustrate the transformation from orange to green, all interventions that build trust among the team members are helpful. Important: this is about human trust among each other, not about trust in processes, key figures, and so on!

The fact that, for example, **individual target agreements** can be **extended by collaborative elements** has already been explained in an earlier example. Other goal-oriented interventions are regular team activities in which the participants **first get to know each other better, free of further intentions.** These can be whole team days, but also smaller activities; for example, meetings with actual orange goals. Through these exercises, the team members learn new things about each other on a personal level and create points of contact beyond the professional level. Step by step, exercises reduce fear and stress in interaction and create green trust and community.

Example: *A project team of an international management consultancy has the task of breaking up its client's previous management practice and introducing lean management. Each team member has their own tasks and responsibilities within the overall project. In order to strengthen the community and to encourage exchange, the team leader has asked each team member to anonymously write down on a piece of paper personal information from their private sphere that the others certainly do not know about yet. At the beginning of each meeting, one of the pieces of paper is read out loud and the team guesses who it is describing. In this way, the team grows closer together from meeting to meeting—and now also knows which of them always eats their pasta with mayonnaise, who used to model, and who composed music that was played in space.*

Green, or actually orange?

As in this example, many classic teambuilding activities often appear green at first glance but are still very much rooted in orange. Although they are designed to create shared experiences, they are a means to an end, to optimize the efficiency and effectiveness of the team. A truly green approach would be to simply have a good time when building a raft together, because the community, detached from Key Figures & Co., has a high value in itself.

From green to yellow

Appreciation, fairness, equality, tolerance, harmony, consensus, and community are some of the characteristic values of a mainly green team culture.

Success is not seen as a short-term achievement from the here and now, but as the result of the right cooperation with the right team composition. In this sense, each member of the group is taken seriously and accepted; their work is highly valued and seen as an important part of the whole.

But **even a green team culture is only ever as appropriate as the team members, the surrounding organization, and/or the market require.**

Example: *The innovation team of a medium-sized mechanical engineering company has been working with brainstorming, design thinking, and creativity techniques for a long time. Many of their ideas have already led to successful product developments. Now the pressure to innovate is increasing. The team is challenged to no longer think "well behaved" but to question things radically. Out of the debate club, into disruptive thinking! According to the motto "You can't do epic shit with normal people," the team members have to become uncomfortable for each other and for others. They are supposed to rip things out of context. In doing so, they are allowed or even supposed to break something—because this is the only way to leave the comfort zone and make yellow revolution instead of evolution possible.*

If green tends to hinder the success of the team, the team members often have endless discussions with no result. Everything is subordinated to the desire for harmony, and there is a lack of implementation power. The strong desire for acceptance and recognition leads to the idea that it is better to do nothing at all than to simply try something out and risk making mistakes. **A yellow desire for independence awakens**—no longer to be thwarted by fixed team structures and the need for unison and harmony, but to flexibly adapt the way of working together depending on the situation and context so that it is efficient and goal oriented. Can corresponding adjustments of the design elements also accelerate the transformation of a mainly green team culture to a yellow one? Clare W. Graves himself says no. In his opinion, **green can be developed only up to the green level. Anything that comes after green simply has to happen.** This is consistent with our experience. Of course, all kinds of measures can be taken to take a green team out of their comfort zone, to shake them up and take them to a new level of cooperation. Ultimately, however, the team must lift itself to the yellow level.

A change in team culture can basically take place in three different ways: on one level, downward, and upward. If the explicit design elements are adapted accordingly and resistance is integrated, the values will adapt in the long term. 30

4.3 Other value-based interventions

The approaches listed so far are based on the explicit design elements: if they are changed, in the long term this also affects the implied values of the team and changes the team culture accordingly.
Another way of developing team culture starts with the values themselves and brings the team **on a meta level into a value-based discussion with itself**. Such a reflection of one's own values causes a team to visualize what it currently considers important and right. On the other hand, it triggers a review of the fit: Is what has long proven itself to the team still what is appropriate for today's challenges and will enable success in the future? In the following we present three value-based interventions:

Us—very typical US!

Each participant (teams of two or three in larger groups) writes down on cards what is typical for the team (one thought per card). Afterward the cards are presented individually—for example, "Everyone talks," "Shape success together," "High quality of results," "One for all, all for one," "Higher, faster, further," "Legendary parties," and "Maintain personal style."
This is followed by an introduction to the Graves model and, if applicable, a presentation of the results of the 9-level analysis. Afterward, the results written at the

beginning are presented. The cards are assigned to a map of the individual levels by the whole group. In case of doubt, the author of the card always has the last word. It is important to question again and again what exactly was meant by the term on the map to get clarity. For example, "Everyone talks" on green could mean that everyone has a say, while on red it means that everyone contributes their opinion unasked and impulsively, ignoring hierarchies.

Usually the result is an image where some levels have many tiles and other levels have few or no tiles. This makes it clear which value level currently predominates. The above-mentioned sample terms on the cards would make it apparent that the team currently has a clear focus on green but that elements of blue, orange, and yellow are also represented.

Experience-based learning

Experience-based learning scenarios are a good way of ensuring that values are not only discussed in the abstract but also experienced firsthand.

For example, a team may be handed a problem that it has to solve together within a given time. Afterward, the participants reflect on their cooperation in this situation: Which core values have been demonstrated and how? How have the participants fared? Were they target oriented for the successful completion of the task? Are there comparable situations, approaches, and ways of thinking in the everyday work of the team? What conclusions can be drawn from the exercise for the future cooperation of the team?

For example, in a workshop with the management team of a medical diagnostics start-up, we used an exercise in which the participants sit blindfolded in a circle and have to solve a puzzle through verbal communication alone. From a set of cards with colors and shapes, the moderator removes two cards and distributes the rest to the participants. If an actor holds up his or her card, the moderator tells him or her the color. The aim of the group is to determine the color and shape of the two missing cards. (Specifically, this is the exercise "KommunikARTio" from METALOG training tools®.)

We have been using this exercise for years in our work with teams—this group was the first to fail to come to a solution. There was a lack of coordination among them and an inability to listen to anyone at all.

Afterward, the participants asked us, "How did we do compared to other teams?" We answered truthfully, "You're the first team ever to really fuck up the exercise." These clear words were chosen deliberately. The team's current score was at the red level, but it should and would move toward the blue. Such a development is fueled by failure. Red is good at grabbing at its honor, its fear of losing face—and accepts blue rules and procedures especially when they promise the greatest success.

Accordingly, great frustration initially spread through the team. The group was angry at itself. They did not enjoy it, but they worked doggedly on a flipchart to work out what had not gone well in the exercise and what would have been useful instead. The next morning we did the exercise again—and the team solved the challenge with flying colors. They experienced that red solutions are not always the best way, opened up to blue approaches, and thus had a sense of achievement.

Prototyping

While experience-based learning makes values emotionally perceptible, prototyping enables people to literally design them with their own hands. Actually, the approach comes from manufacturing and software development and has the goal of first trying out new processes by means of low-cost, inexpensive test versions. We like to take such an approach, for example, when a team comes together for the first time or is facing major changes. Through prototyping, the new culture can first be developed in the model and then viewed and tested from all sides to see if and how the individual elements fit together harmoniously.

For this purpose we provide the participants with a large amount of material. Building blocks, handicraft materials, plasticine—no matter what, the main thing is a lot and as varied as possible. (Highly recommendable for this are, for example, the building kits of LEGO® Serious Play®.)

You are given the task: "Create a model with the existing material. What should your team culture look like so that you can work together and be fit for the future? Which big pictures, but also small details, will be important?" After the construction phase by individuals or in small groups, the participants present their prototypes to the whole group. A workshop with a car dealership's sales team, for example, focused on how they can better achieve their orange growth targets in the future. Because the manufacturer had terminated their contract, the entire dealership had to reposition itself. In small groups, the participants used building blocks to work out how they imagine their ideal future car dealership. When the results were presented, it became clear that each small group had built in many green elements: open doors and broken barriers for the customers, antennas for their needs, flowers for well-being, King Customer in the center, and so on. It became clear that although orange targets were still in the foreground (there were coins, treasure chests, safes, etc. everywhere), the team felt a certain pressure to change toward green. Afterward, the team jointly considered which measures they would like to take in order to actually initiate and successfully realize a cultural change from pure orange to orange-green.

Many other possibilities

Of course, there are many more exercises and approaches to enable teams to reflect on their culture and adaptation through value-based interventions—they do not have to be based on the Graves model. In order to be effective, it is not the concrete method itself that is important, but that it fits the current team culture, is accepted by the team, and does not cause too much resistance.

We hope that we were able to give you some ideas for reflection as well as suggestions for culture and value work that fits perfectly into your team context. We wish you valuable experiences and results!

30

Changing conditions may require a change in team culture. This can be at one level, but also toward a level below or above. Value-based interventions are another way to develop team culture. Various exercises, such as prototyping or experience-based learning, encourage the team to consciously reflect on its values, and trigger changes.

Fast reader

1. The importance of team culture

The efficient cooperation of teams is becoming increasingly important in modern organizations. In a time of rapid and increasing specialization, many heads (and hands) are needed to meet the demands of the working world. But teamwork does not always lead to better results. Often the reason for the failure of teams is a lack of fit between individuals, groups, organizations, and/or the market. Only when these four elements are in harmony can a team really work successfully.

Team culture ***refers to all the factors that make up the team at its core and determine its cooperation and interaction with the environment. It is shaped by the individuals but also by external influences.***

2. Elements of team culture

Following the 7-S model, we distinguish seven design elements of team culture. The six explicit design elements and one implicit design element are the levers with which team culture can be shaped and changed.

The seven design elements are as follows:

- ***Staff: Each team member contributes with his or her personality, experience, and skills.*** 30
- ***Style: In addition to the management style, communication patterns as well as recognition and sanction mechanisms play a role here.***
- ***Skills: Communication, dealing with mistakes, and so on determine the overall performance of the team.***
- ***Systems: This includes all tools and instruments with which a team achieves its added value. The processes can have different levels of maturity.***
- ***Structure: This refers to the organizational units in the team that determine who gets what information and decisions from whom and passes them on to whom.***
- ***Strategy: This includes the long-term goals or vision and what concrete measures are taken to achieve them.***
- ***Shared values: These define what the team***

considers right or wrong and are reflected in the design of the other six elements.

3. Stages of team culture

Values are the implicit foundation of every team culture. They are never right or wrong but always more or less appropriate to the individual team member, the organization surrounding the team, and the market in which the team operates. Values are not static; they change.
Psychology professor Clare W. Graves first demonstrated in the 1960s that there are specific patterns according to which value systems develop in stages. The 9 Levels of Value Systems by Rainer Krumm is a simplification and further development of Graves's theory. Using scientifically valid questionnaires, it makes visible how the value levels of individuals, teams, and organizations are developed and interact as a value system.

30 ***As an implicit design element, each value level is linked to a specific design of the explicit elements of team culture:***

- ***Purple—Values: tradition, obedience, commitment. Characteristic: exclusive decision-making power of the superior.***
- ***Red—Values: power, courage, strength. Char-***

acteristics: authoritarian leadership, enormous power, competition among employees.

- ***Blue—Values: quality, discipline, loyalty. Characteristics: dutiful employees, strictly hierarchical structure, clearly regulated processes.***
- ***Orange—Values: performance, productivity. Characteristic: continuous optimization of processes.***
- ***Green—Values: cooperation, appreciation, community. Characteristic: fast integration of new members.***
- ***Yellow—Values: multiperspectivity, independence, further development. Characteristics: group structured as a loose network rather than a team, hierarchies do not play a role.***
- ***Turquoise—Values: sustainability, collective intuition, global reconciliation. This level has only recently emerged. So far there are hardly any examples of turquoise teams.***

4. Development of team culture

In a world that is constantly changing, the team culture must also be constantly reoriented. However, changes can also cause resistance. For a successful transformation, it is important to recognize these and to productively incorporate them into the change process. A change process can basically take place in three different ways: on one level, back to the previous level, and upward to the next level.

30 ***Such a transformation can be actively initiated and controlled by consciously changing the explicit elements of team culture. Typical transformations:***

- ***Blue to orange: A blue team is used to managing correctly but on demand—but now needs to be proactive. Slowness, rigidity, and inflexibility must be replaced by innovation and entrepreneurial thinking.***
- ***Orange to green: An orange team can tilt toward greed, strong competition, and high-performance pressure, leading to a desire for green.***
- ***Green to yellow: When team members no longer want to be held back by the green need for harmony, a yellow desire for independence, flexibility, and goal orientation awakens.***

Another possibility for developing team culture is value-based interventions at the level of classical team development.

The authors

Rainer Krumm, managing director of the 9 Levels Institute for Value Systems and axiocon GmbH, is a management trainer, consultant, coach, and author. He has advised international companies, managers, and teams in over 23 countries. He is considered one of the most experienced consultants and trainers in the field of corporate culture and change management—based on the developmental psychology of Prof. Clare W. Graves. With the 9 levels he has developed an analysis tool that makes value systems tangible and measurable.

Sonja Wittig is managing director of 9 Levels Germany and co-owner of the Institute for Personality. As a trainer, systemic coach, team developer, and consultant with many years of experience in HR management, she supports individuals, teams, and organizations in achieving their goals with values-based interventions and also trains others to use the 9 levels.

www.9levels. de
www.9levels.com

Related literature

- Burke, Kelly (2011): In teamwork, one bad apple really does make a difference. Sydney Morning Herald, 27.06.2011; https://www.smh.com.au/lifestyle/in-teamwork-one-bad-apple-really-does-make-a-difference-20110626-1glug.html
- Graves, Clare W.: Deterioration of Work Standards. Harvard Business Review, 44(5), 1966, S. 117–128
- Krumm, Rainer: 9 Levels of Value Systems. Ein Entwicklungsmodell für die Persönlichkeitsentfaltung und die Evolution von Organisationen und Kulturen. Werdewelt Verlags- und Medienhaus GmbH, 3. Auflage 2017
- Krumm, Rainer: 30 Minuten Werteorientiertes Führen. GABAL, 3. Auflage 2014
- Krumm, Rainer; Martina Bär-Sieber; Hartmut Wiehle: Unternehmen verstehen, gestalten, verändern. Das Graves-Value-System in der Praxis. Springer Gabler, 3. Auflage 2015
- Metz-Göckel, Hellmuth (2003): Psychologie der Gruppe. Technische Universität Dortmund, 31.01.2003; https://eldorado.tu-dortmund.de/bitstream/2003/2953/1/Psychologie.pdf
- Piccard, Bertrand: Spuren am Himmel. Piper, 2003
  Rettig, Daniel; Lin Freitag; Jan Guldner; Kristin Schmidt (2017): Ich Team, du Work. Wirtschafts-Woche 48, 17.11.2017, S. 19–24

Index

7-S model 4, 8, 15ff., 87
9 Levels of Value Systems 4, 18, 39ff., 88, 92

Beck, Don 38

Change direction 4, 71ff.
Change pressure 7, 37, 44, 69ff., 84
Cowan, Christopher 38
Culture 9, 14, 83ff., 91

Employees 4, 6, 14, 17, 20, 22ff., 46ff., 71f., 89
Experience-based learning 81, 83, 85

Fit 4, 8, 13ff., 69, 75, 80, 83ff.

Graves, Clare W. 4, 7, 32, 36ff., 44, 63, 79f., 84, 88
Group Value System 42ff.

Maturity level of processes 29f., 53, 56, 87
New Work 21

Personal Value System 40-45
Potential 11ff., 27, 41
Prototyping 83, 85
Processes 4, 6, 17, 28ff., 47ff., 72ff., 83, 87, 89

resistance to change 4, 70
Resistance to value level 40ff.
Ringman effect 12

Skills 4, 6, 14, 16ff., 34, 44, 47ff., 87
Spiral Dynamics 39
Strategy 44, 48, 51, 53ff., 60, 64f., 87
Structure 4, 6, 16ff., 30f., 34, 44, 48, 51, 53, 56, 59ff., 87, 89

Team (definition) 10
Team development 72, 90
Transformation 70, 72, 74, 76, 79, 89

Value-based intervention 68, 82ff.
Values 6, 16ff., 33ff.
Value analysis 18
Vision and Mission 32
VUCA 69